Grey seals have a long dog-like snout (nose) with wide **nostrils**. Adults can be up to 2.5 metres long.

In this book we will be looking mostly at grey seals. **Male** grey seals have dark brown-grey hair with light patches. **Females** are lighter with dark patches.

Where seals live

Grey seals usually swim underwater for about ten minutes at a time. Then they come up to breathe air.

Seals spend most of their lives in the sea. They swim and feed underwater but they need to come to the surface to breathe.

Contents

Any words appearing in the text in bold, **like this**, are explained in the Glossary.

What are seals?

Common seals, like these, are smaller than grey seals. Their coats are more spotted and their heads are rounder.

Seals are **mammals** that live in the sea. There are two kinds of seal that live around Britain – the grey seal and the common seal.

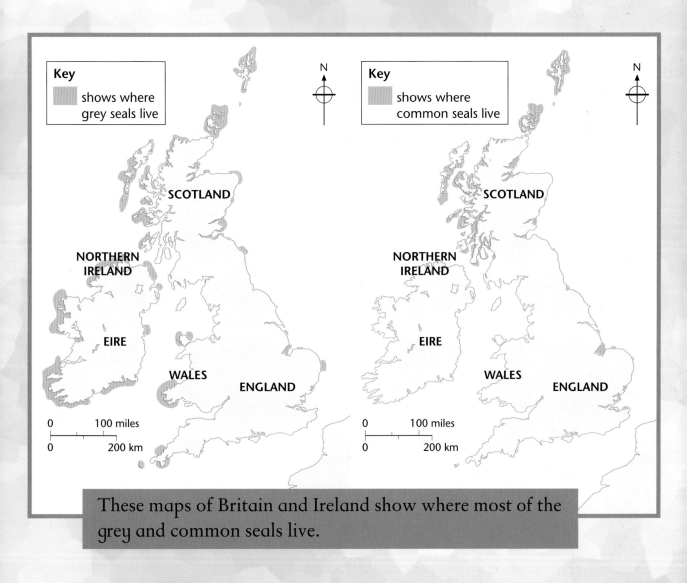

SCOTLAND

NORTHERN IRELAND

EIRE

WALES

ENGLAND

0   100 miles

0   200 km

SCOTLAND

NORTHERN IRELAND

EIRE

WALES

ENGLAND

0   100 miles

0   200 km

These maps of Britain and Ireland show where most of the grey and common seals live.

Seals come ashore to rest between feeding trips. They also come ashore to have their young. Grey seals **haul out** on islands, rocky shores and in caves.

7

What seals eat

Grey seals catch their food in the water.

Seals are carnivores. This means they eat other animals. Grey seals mainly feed on fish, such as cod, herring and sand eels. They eat crabs and squid, too.

flipper

Seals sometimes hold food with their front flippers.

Seals swallow small fish whole. They hold
larger fish in their front **flippers** and bite
bits off to eat. Grey seals sometimes eat sea
birds that they find swimming on the sea.

Finding food

A seal's large eyes help it to spot fish deep under water where it is dark.

Seals usually find fish by seeing them or hearing them. Seals have tiny ear holes at the sides of the head. Their whiskers feel movements that tell them fish are nearby.

When a seal spots a fish, it rushes forward to catch it.

Seals may swim a long way to find food. They often dive down as deep as 70 metres to catch fish. When they dive, seals close their **nostrils** and hold their breath.

11

On the move

A seal's smooth, sausage-shaped body helps it move through the water quickly.

Seals swim by flapping their back **flippers** up and down. They use their front flippers for steering. The five 'fingers' on each flipper are **webbed** to push against the water.

Seals sometimes use their front flippers to balance themselves when moving on land.

Seals glide through the water but they are rather slow and clumsy on land. To move on rocks or sand, a seal holds up its back flippers and bumps along on its belly.

Resting

Seals keep their noses poking out of the water when they sleep so they can breathe.

Seals can rest while they are in the water.
They close their eyes and sleep upright,
like a large bottle floating at the surface.

Seals rarely swim far from their favourite rocks to feed.

Grey seals often visit rocky shores to rest and sleep. Only some places are good to **haul out** on. Most grey seals have favourite caves or rocks for resting.

15

Seal groups

In the breeding season, **males** come ashore to **mate** with females.

Grey seals meet in groups when they come ashore to rest. They also meet on the shore in the **breeding season**.

Hundreds of female seals may gather in one place.

Females gather together to give birth to their **pups** (baby seals). After the pups have been born, there may be hundreds of mothers and babies in one place.

Seal young

A pup's white hair keeps it warm until it has grown a layer of fat called **blubber**.

Mother seals usually give birth to one **pup** each year. When a grey seal pup is born it is covered in furry white hair.

Seal pups may suckle five or six times a day, for about ten minutes at a time.

Seal pups feed on their mother's milk, just like other young **mammals**. This milk is rich in fat so the pups grow quickly. Pups **suckle** for the first two or three weeks of their life.

Growing up

This seal pup is moulting. By the time it is four weeks old it will have a coat of short hair, like an adult.

When pups are three weeks old, their mothers swim away. The pups look after themselves now. Their white hair **moults**. It falls out and adult hair grows in its place.

This young seal is making its first trip out to sea. When it is four or five years old it may have young of its own.

The pups are fat enough to live without much food for a while. They swim near the beach and catch some fish. By six weeks old they can hunt far out at sea.

Seal sounds

Some people say that when a seal pup cries it sounds like a human baby crying.

Seals use sounds to tell each other things, like when they are hungry or angry. Pups whine or make high bleating sounds to tell their mother they are hungry.

Adult **males** and **females** make similar noises, but males make deeper sounds.

Adult seals moan to tell another seal to keep away if it gets too close. They snarl when they are angry at another seal or if they are afraid of something.

Under attack

Killer whales, like this one, may catch seals around Britain when they swim far out to sea.

Seals are large and fast, so there are few other animals that eat them. Sharks and killer whales catch some grey seals in the sea around Britain.

Males usually die younger than females because of injuries from fights.

Male seals sometimes attack each other. They fight over **females** when it is time to **mate**. Many females live to about 35 years old, but males only live to about age 25.

Dangers

Four out of every ten seal pups do not make it to their first birthday.

Seal **pups** face many dangers. They may be thrown against rocks by waves or drowned in rough seas. Sometimes their mothers leave them early and they starve.

This seal has an old fishing net tangled around its neck.
Without help, it may die.

Pups and adult seals are sometimes killed
when they get tangled in old fishing nets.
Some are **poisoned** by oil that washes into
their caves from ships at sea.

A seal's year

Male and female grey seals meet each year to **mate**. The new pup that grows inside the female is born a year later.

Adult seals spend most of their year alone at sea. They come ashore in autumn to have **pups**.

Adult grey seals moult their coat of hair every spring.

Each spring, grey seals **moult**. At first the new hair that grows is thin and cool for summer. By winter, it is thick enough to keep them warm in the cold sea.

Animal groups

Scientists group together animals that are alike. Seals are grouped with sea lions and walruses. They are all big **mammals** that live and feed mostly in the sea.

Grey seal

Sea lion

Walrus

The artwork on this page is not to scale.

Glossary

blubber   thick layer of fat under a mammal's skin that helps to keep it warm

breeding season   time when males and females come together to mate

female   animal which can become a mother when it is grown up. A female human is called a woman or a girl.

flipper   wide and flat arm or leg of a sea animal like a seal, used for swimming

haul out   when seals come ashore

male   animal which can become a father when it is grown up. A male human is called a man or a boy.

mammals   group of animals that includes humans. All mammals feed their babies on their own milk and have some hair on their bodies.

mate   what a male and female animal do to start a baby growing inside the female

moult   when an animal loses its old coat of hair ready to grow a new one

nostrils   nose holes

poisoned   when an animal takes something into its body that harms it

pup   baby seal

scientist   person who studies the world around us and the things in it to find out how they work

suckle   when a mother feeds her baby with milk from her body

webbed   when an animal has skin between its fingers or toes. Webbed hands or feet help an animal to swim faster.

Index